Just Beachy
ADULT COLORING BOOKS
By Beth Ingrias

Want to color more for FREE?

Get a FREE 25 page adult coloring book

visit

www.BethIngrias.com

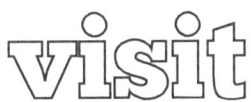

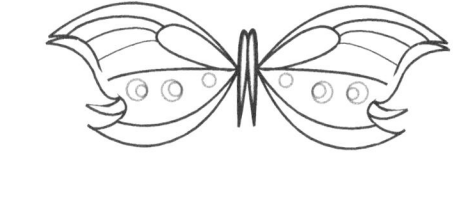

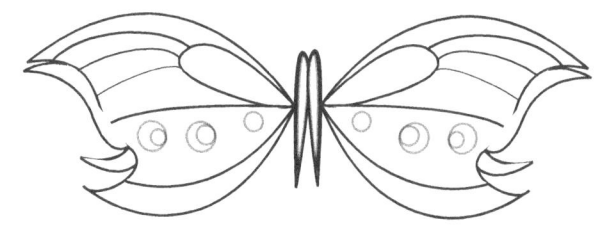

ISBN-13: 978-1-945803-00-0
ISBN-10: 1-945803-00-2

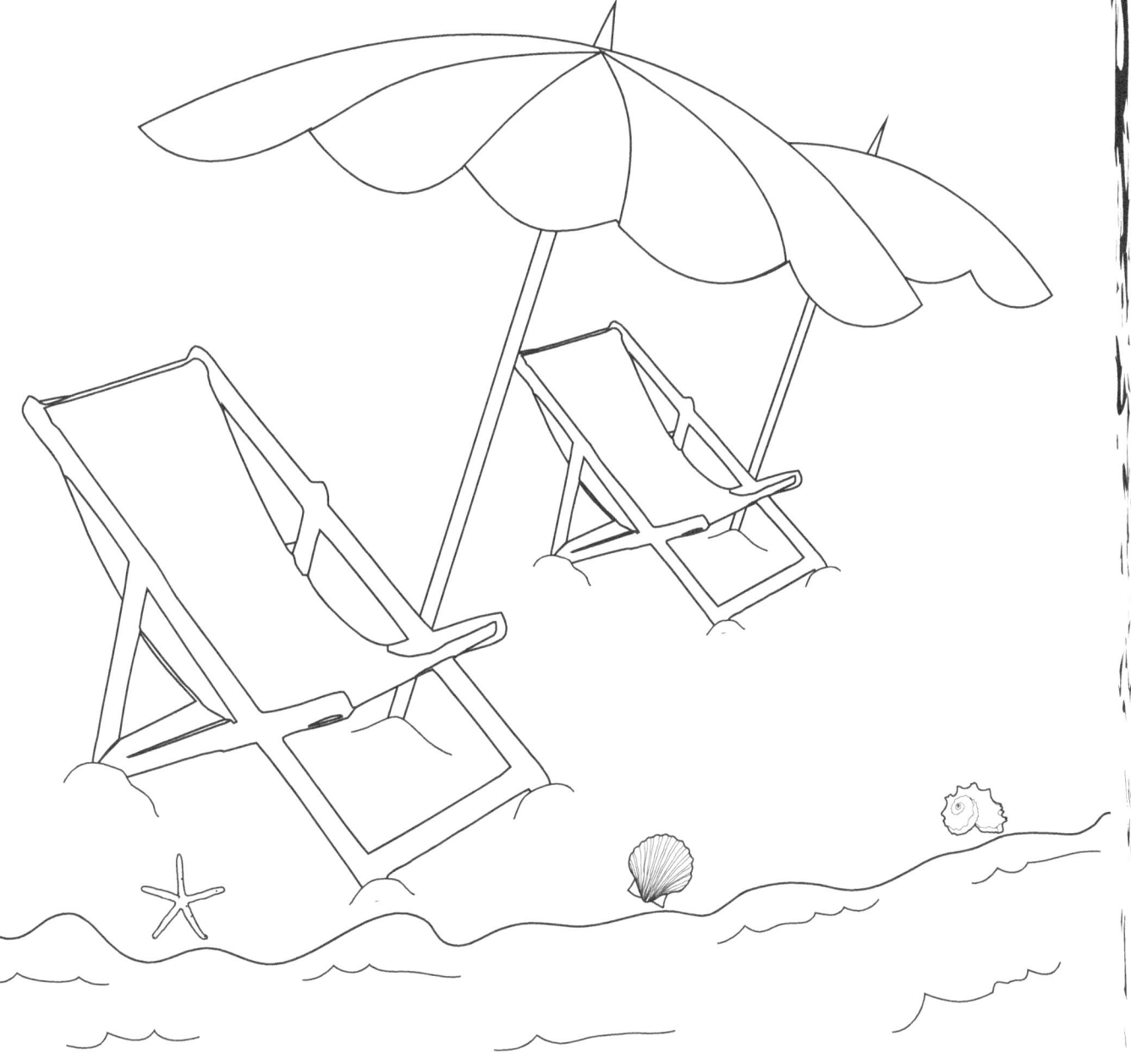

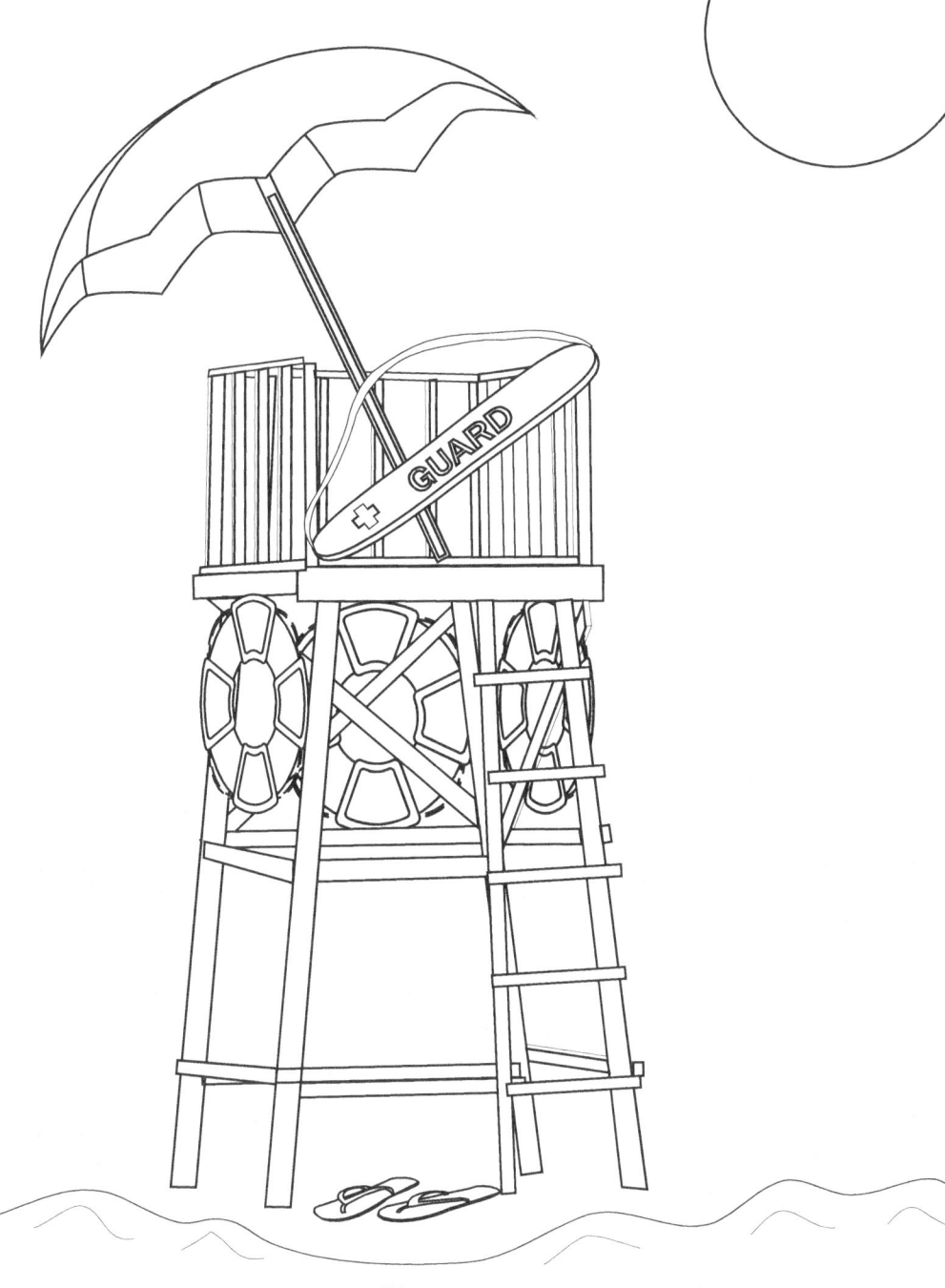

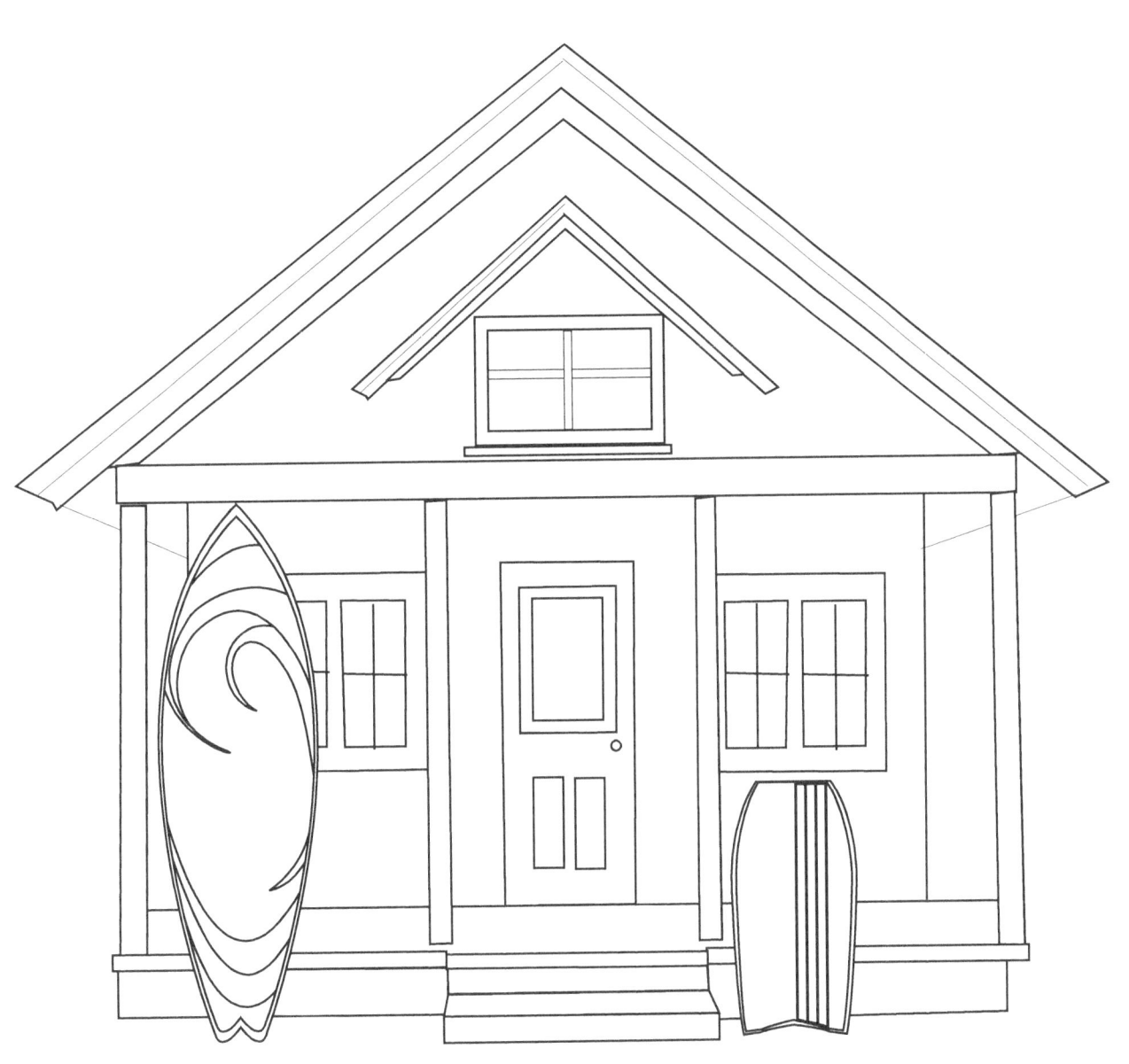

Beach house
life is better here

Happiness is walking on the beach

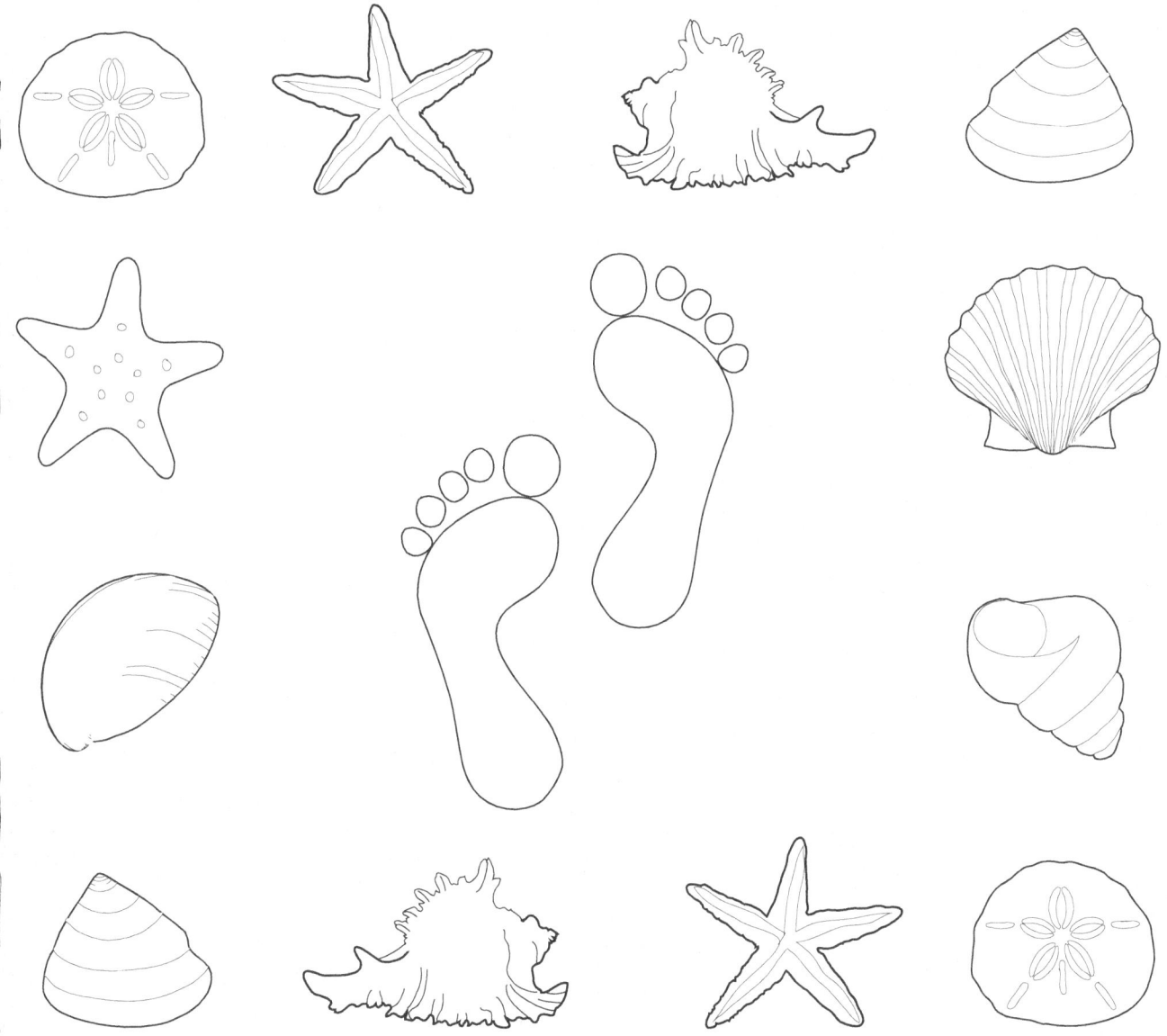

Flip Flop
state of mind

All I need is a healthy dose of vitamin sea

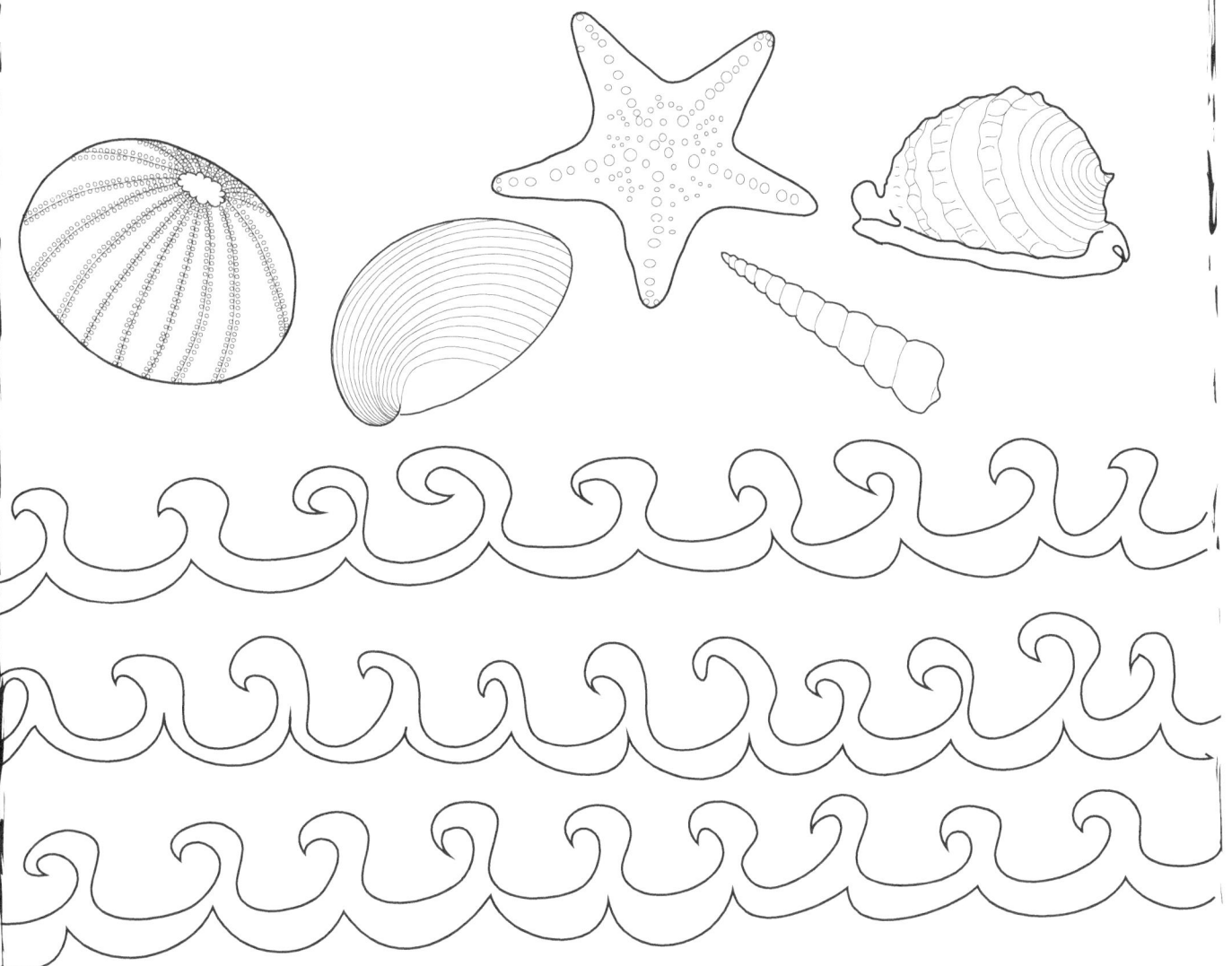

Channel your inner mermaid

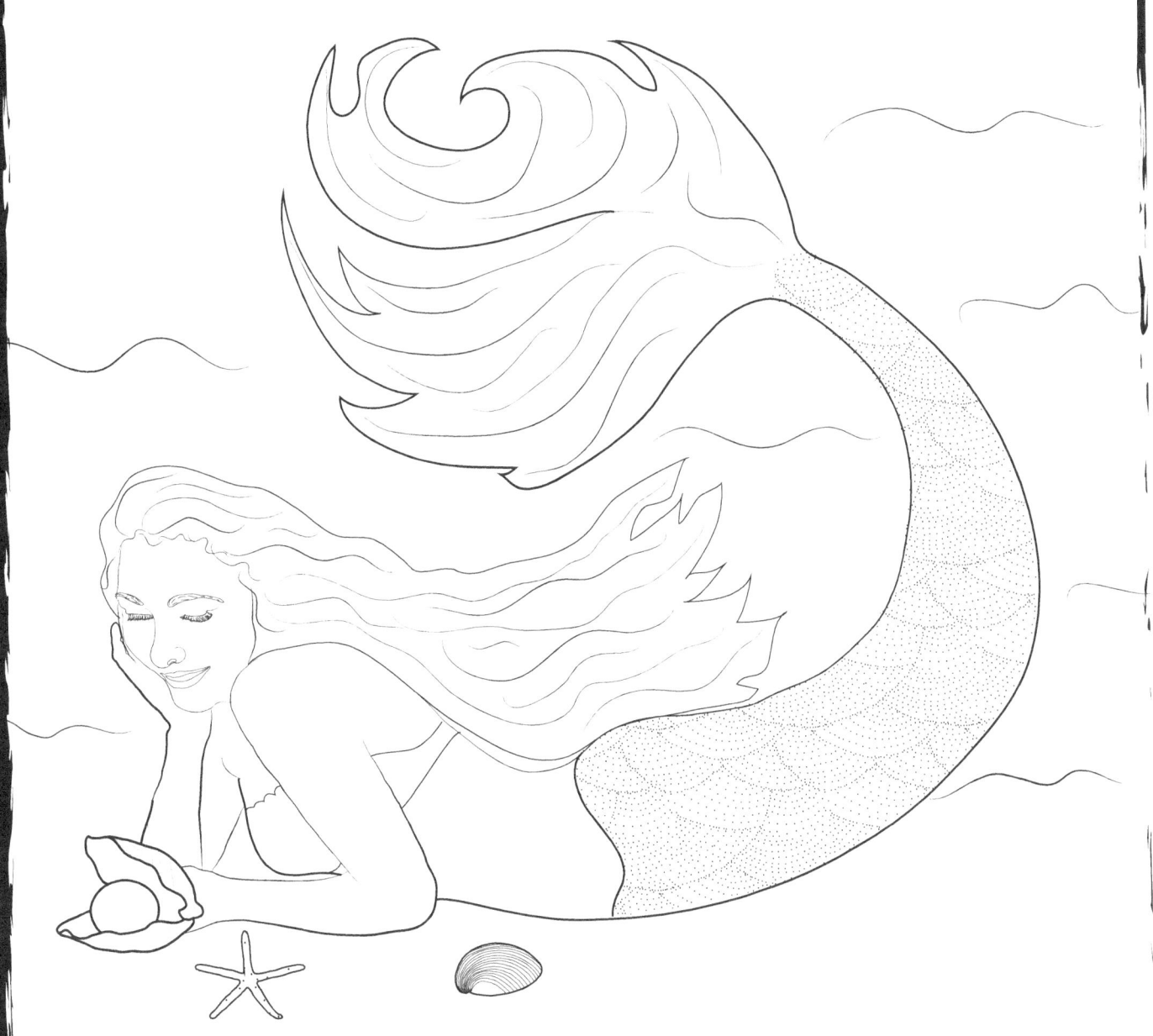

My happy place

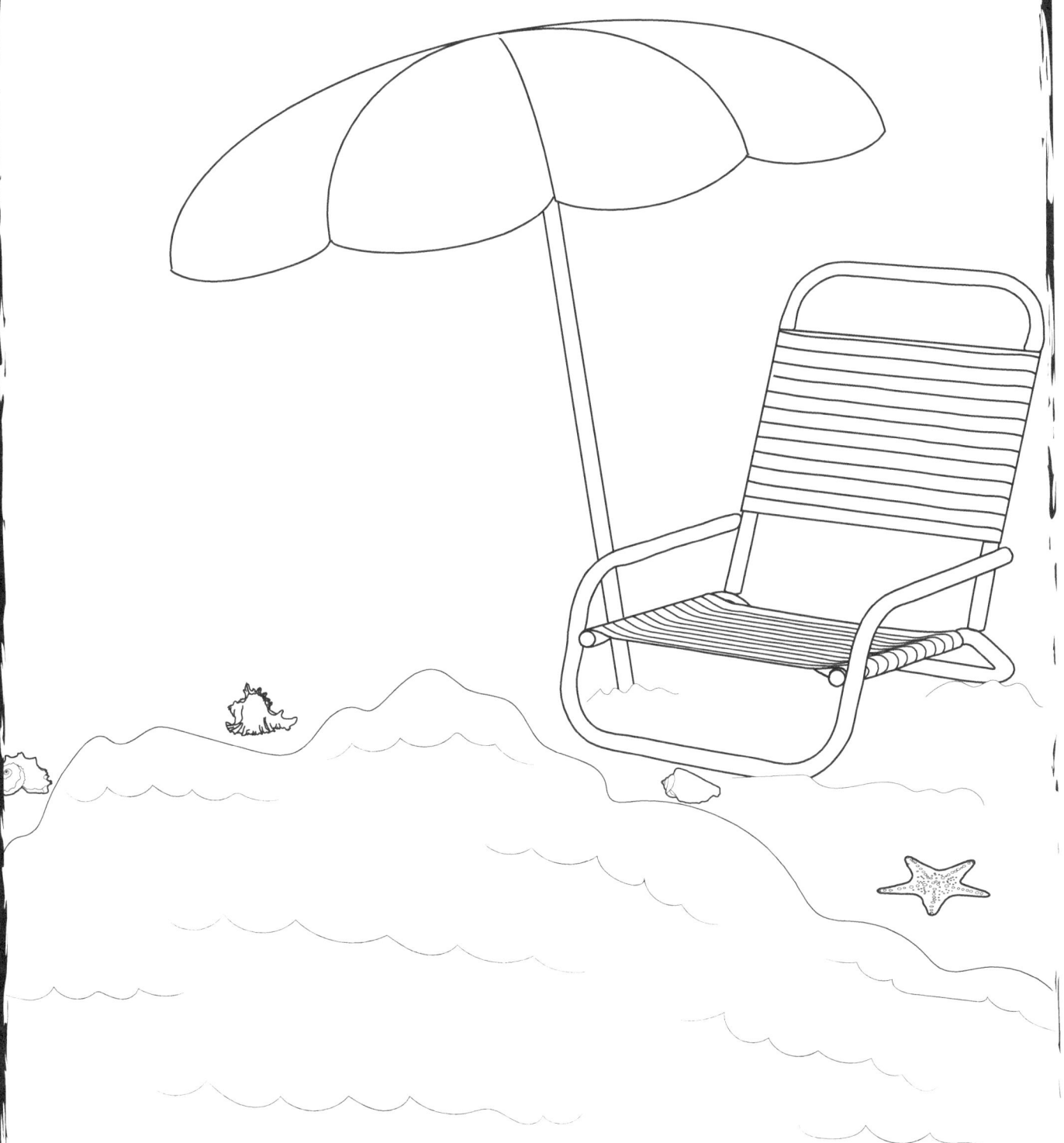

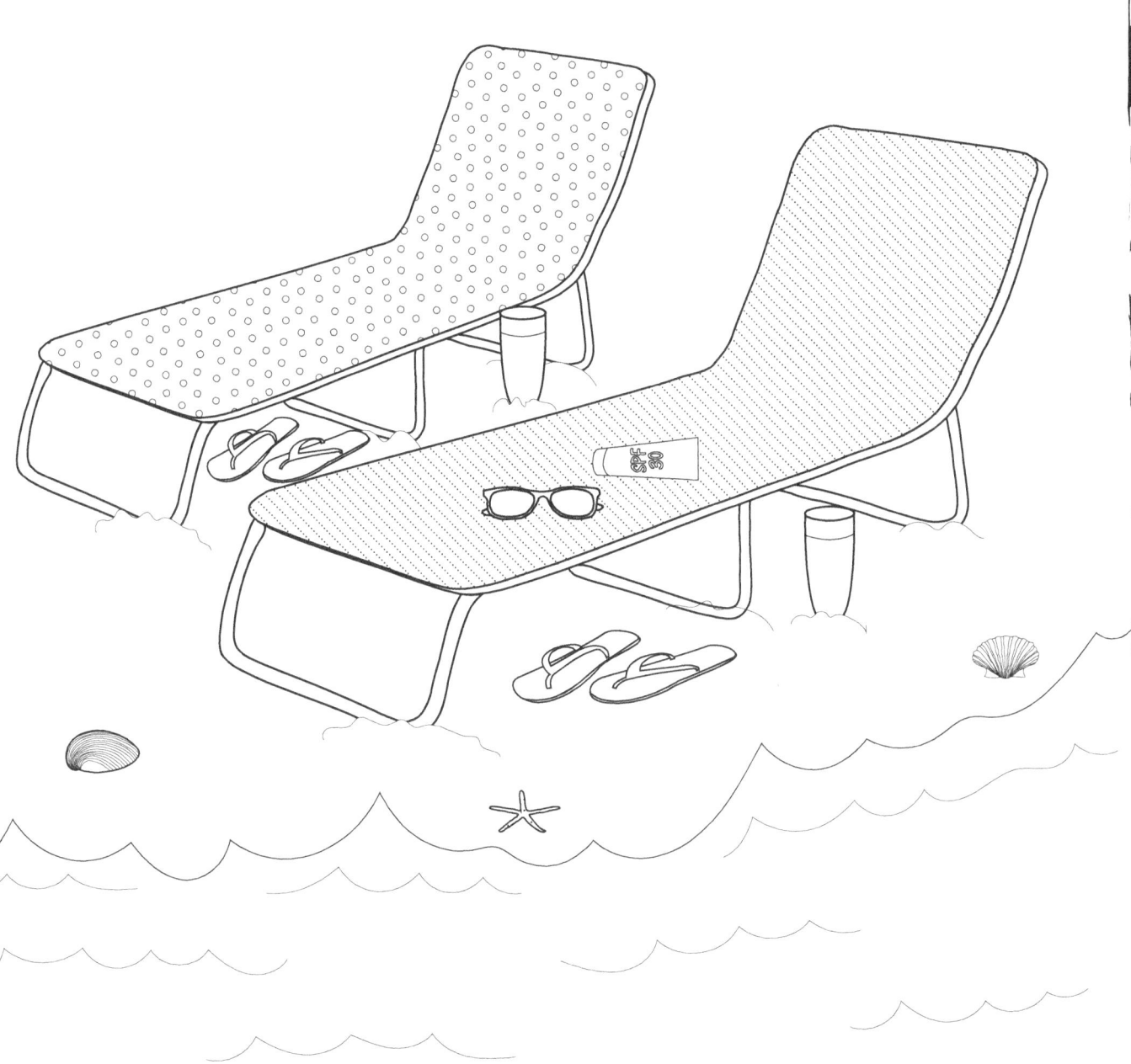

A good day ends with sandy toes

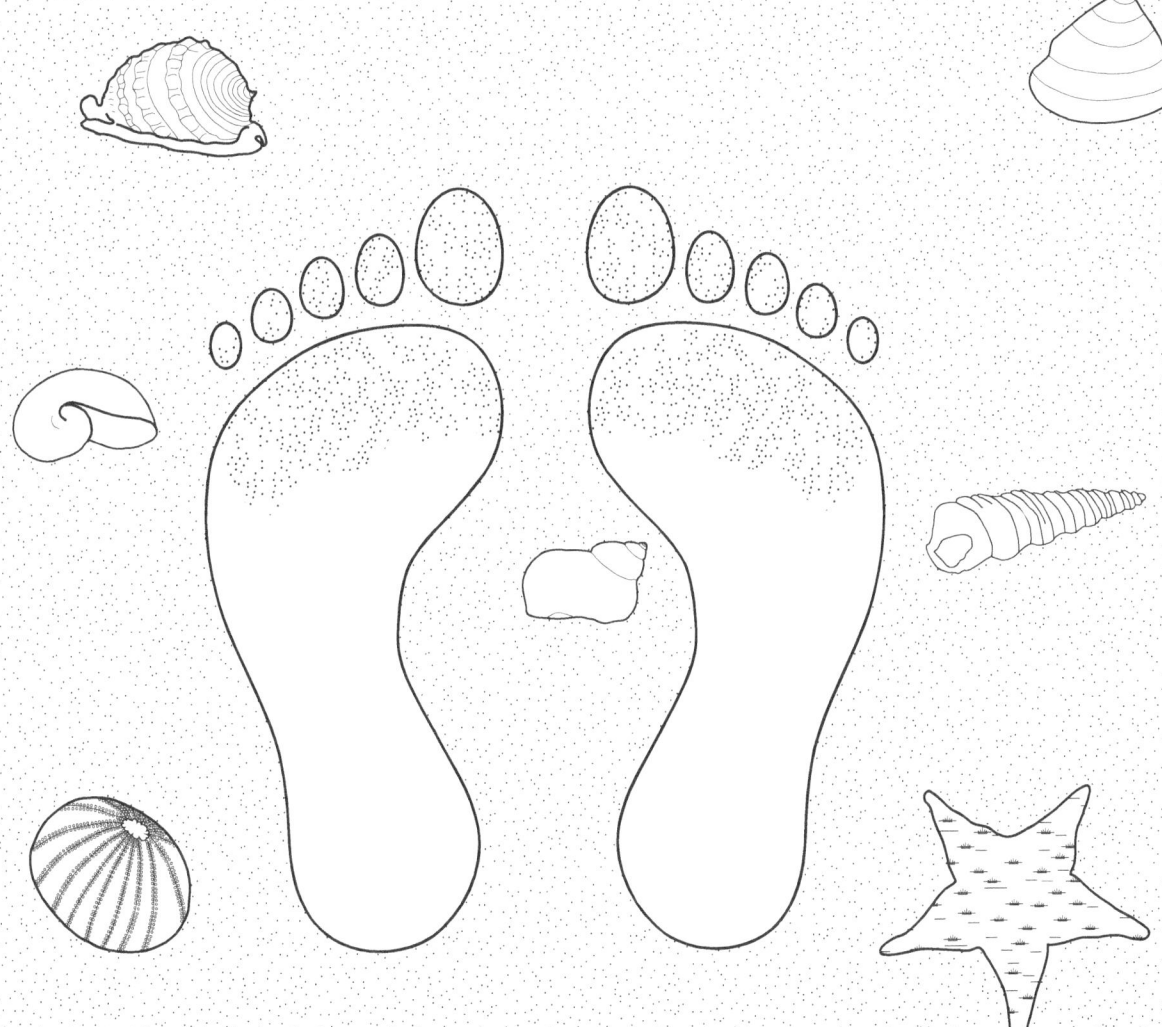

The sun, the sand
and a drink in my hand

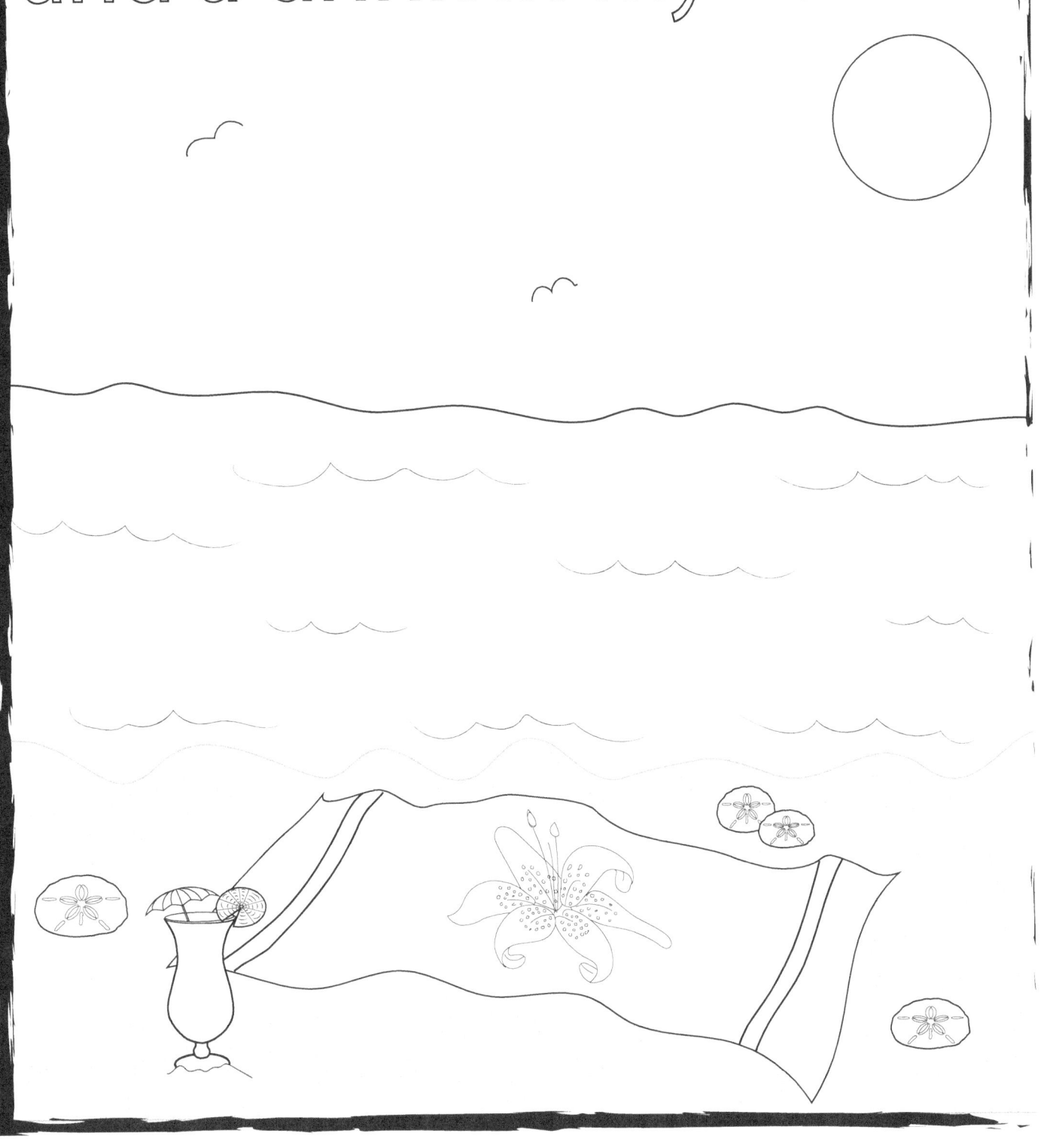

salty kisses

and

mermaid
wishes

Surf
Sand
Sun

The sea is a dolphin's playground

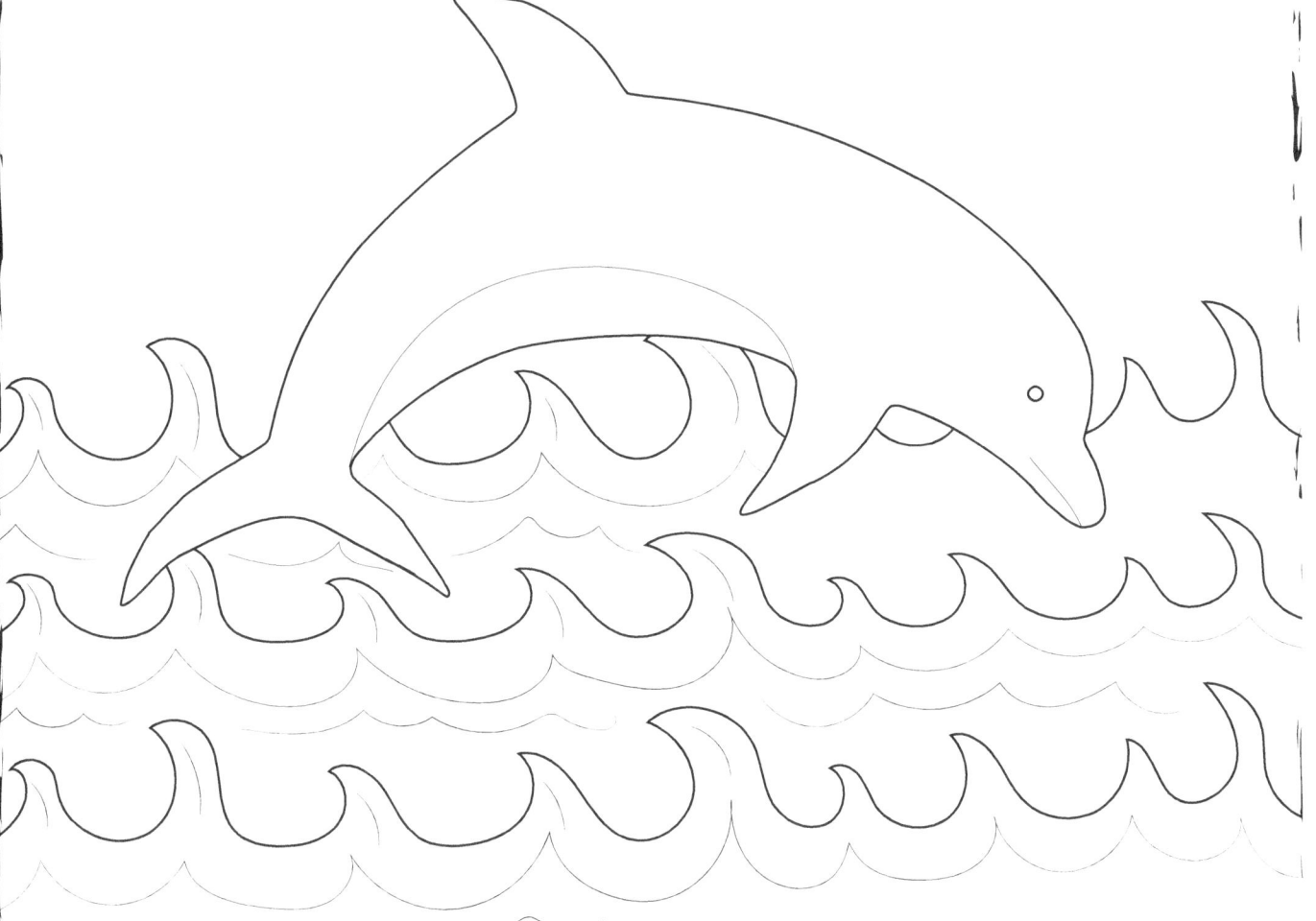

Sand beneath our feet

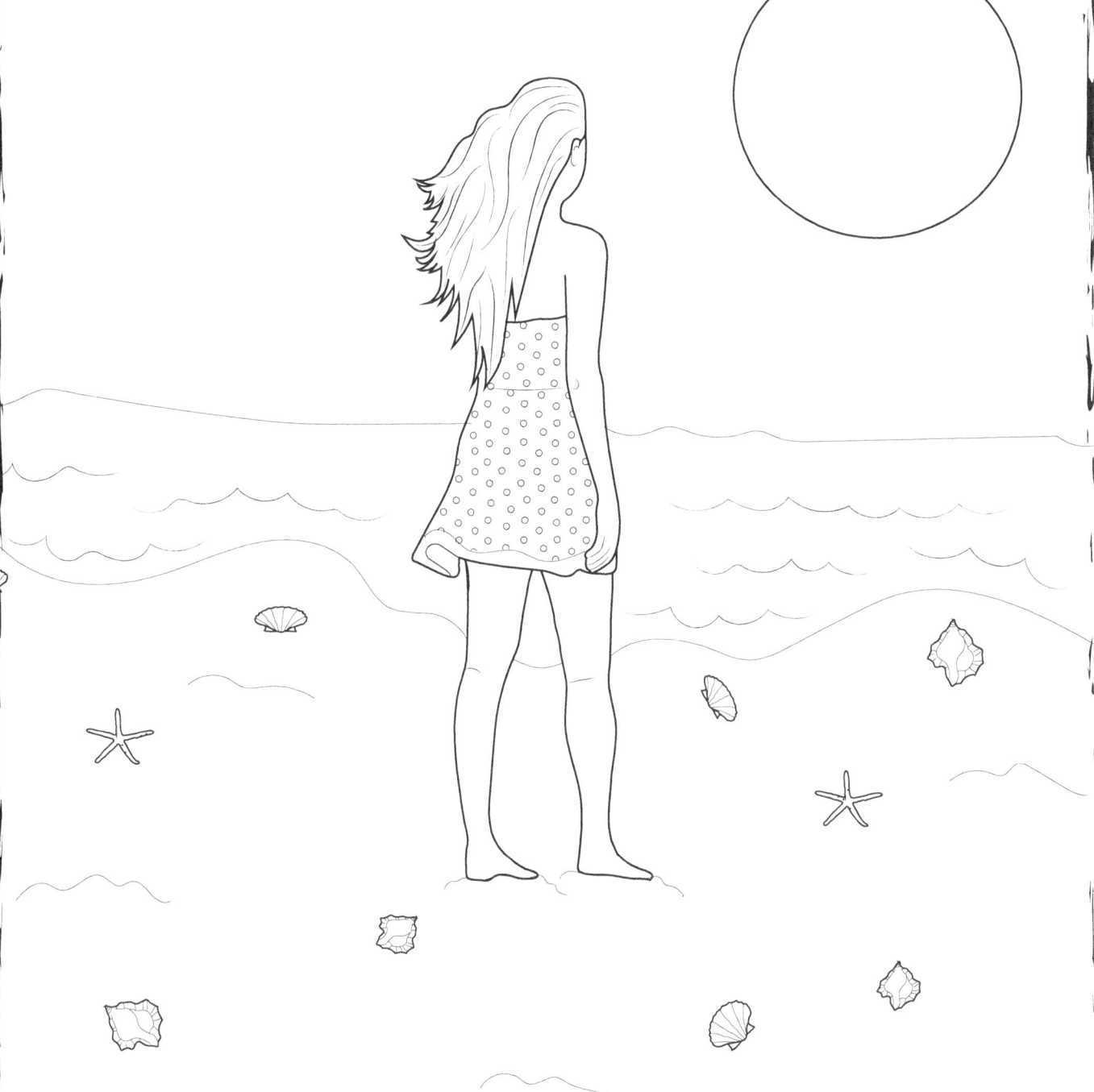

Living on island time.

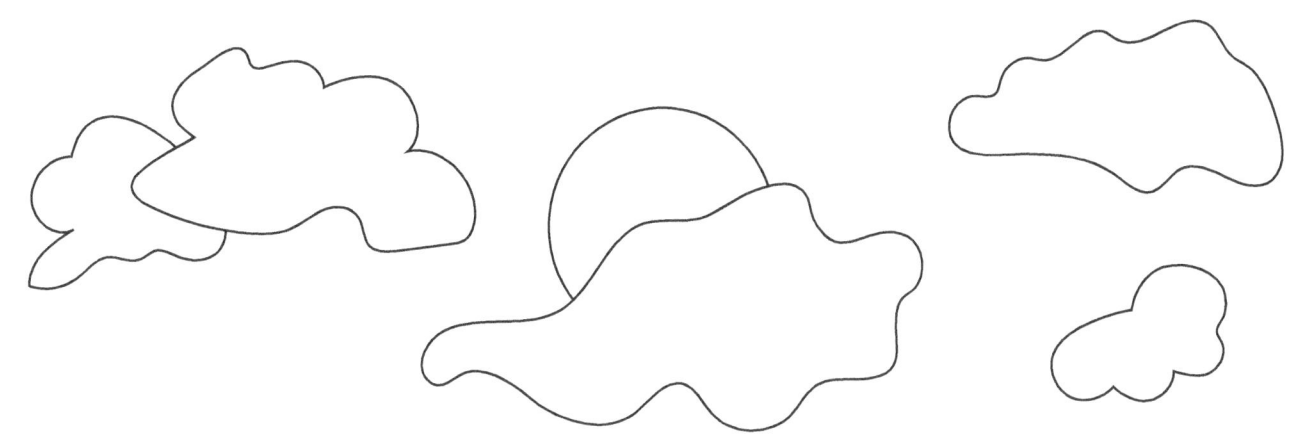

May all your blues
be the ocean
and the sea

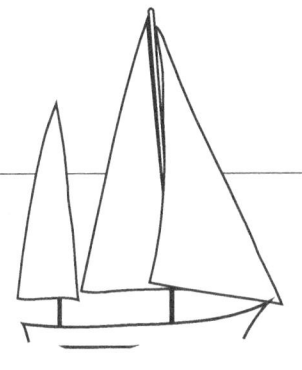

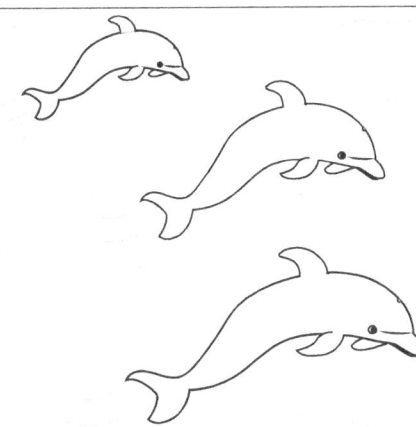

If I were royalty
I would want my castle
by the sea

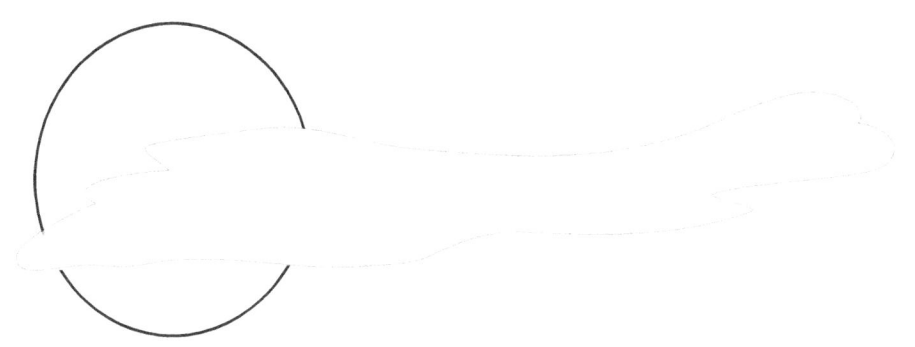

CRASHING WAVES AND A STARLIT SKY

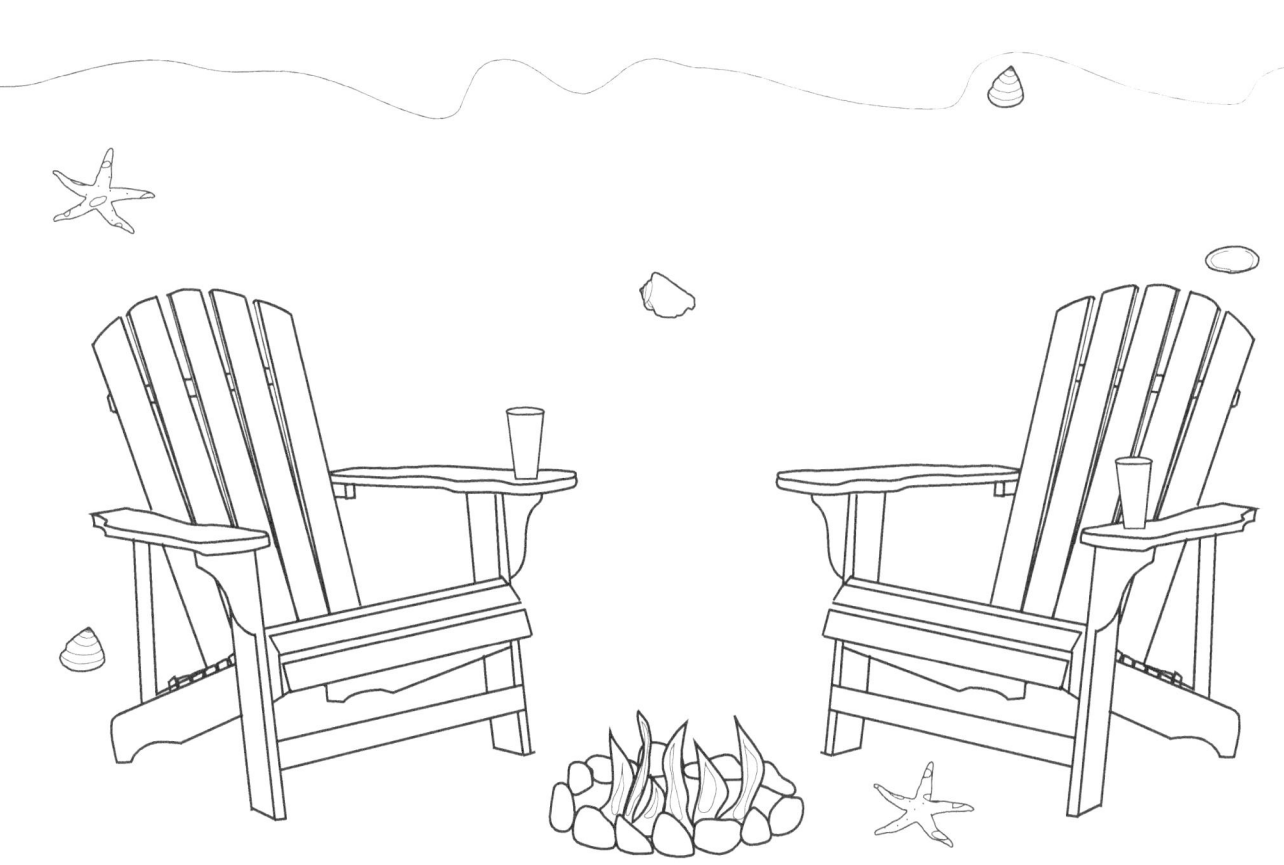

Every day should be a beach day

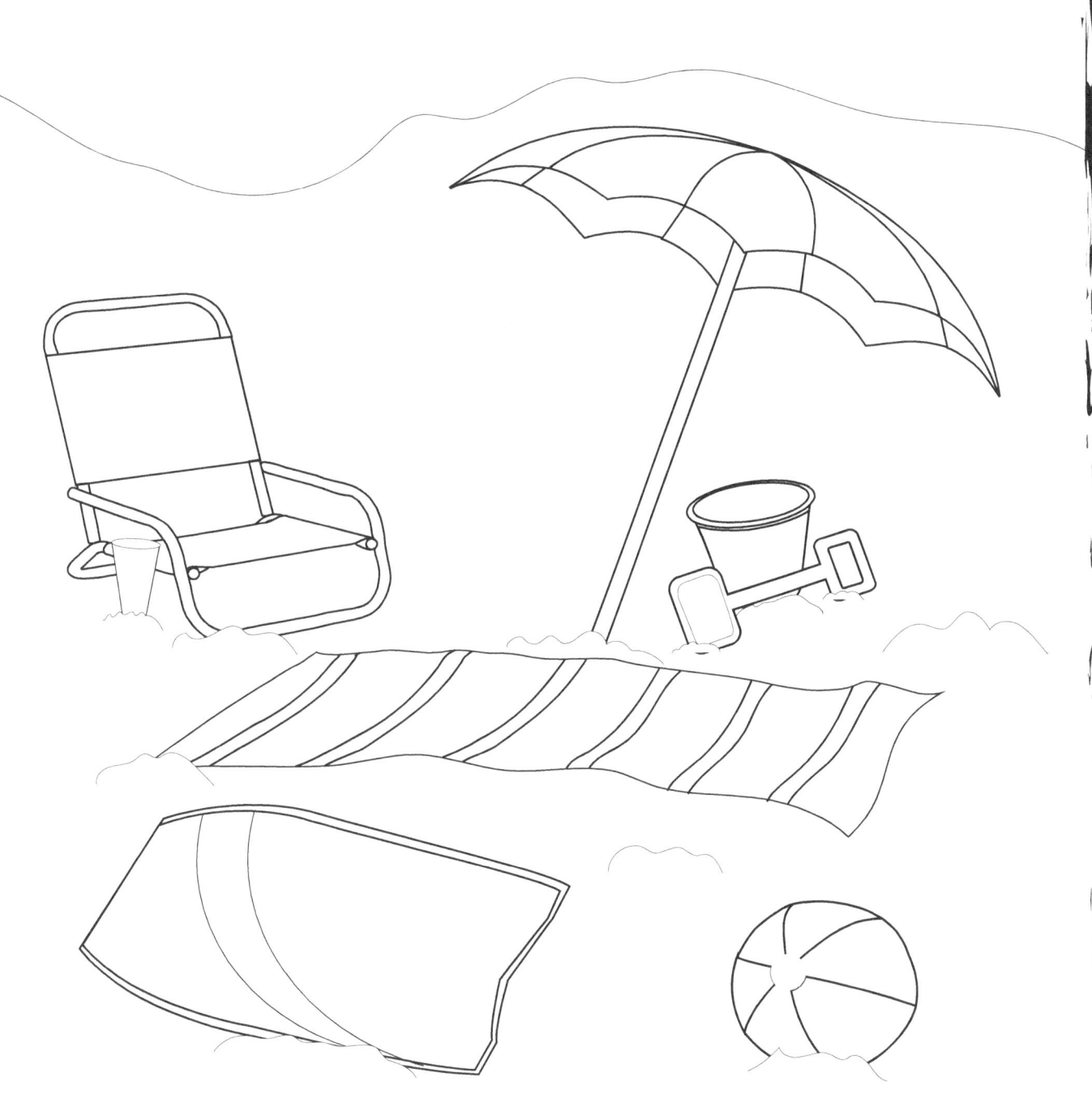

Thanks for picking up a copy of my book. I really appreciate it. If you enjoyed coloring these pages please feel free to leave a review! I would love to hear what you think of my designs.

I would also love to see how you have chosen to color some of my designs. Feel free to email me some pictures of the pages you have colored. You can email me here:

bethingrias@gmail.com

Thanks,
Beth

P.S.
Don't forget to get your free 25 page coloring book at my website.

www.bethingrias.com

www.ingramcontent.com/pod-product-compliance
Lightning Source LLC
Chambersburg PA
CBHW082009230526

45468CB00023B/2991